The Self-Motivation Workbook for Restaurant Employees

The Customer Engagement & Sales Workbook for Restaurant Employees.

The Guide To Success, Higher Tips and More Sales and Job Fulfillment Post Covid

Read this to Increase Money, Customers and Positive On-line Reviews While Reducing Effort, Work and Hours!

New to the industry or seasoned pro this workbook is designed to help you to get more value from each and every hour and each and every customer interaction you have.

A new perspective on an age old industry, these chapters and tools were designed specifically to help you fall in love with customer service again and get much much more from your words, the business you work for, your neighborhood, customers, co-workers and more!

I hope you enjoy and make much more money!

Use These Tips, Tricks and Tools To Create More Money and More Customers and Opportunities ....Fast!

This One Of A Kind Hospitality / Customer Service Program Is Designed To Increase Income and Save Time and Energy. It Also Will Create: Customers, Bigger Tips, More Restaurant Profits, Better Customer Satisfaction And More Customer Engagement, Higher Social Media Exposure, Frequent Message Branding And Amazing Employee Team Spirit.

Read Entirely For Guaranteed Better Results And Higher Sales.

CONTENTS AND WORKBOOK

Chapter 1:

Employees vs. Superstars

Waiters if you are pursuing other interests outside of the restaurant then you are also a business owner for those other endeavors. The chapters for "Restaurant Owners/Managers" are an excellent resource for you as a small business owner as well.

In the following chapters though, you will learn to create customer experiences and engagements which will have your customers on their best behavior and coming back for more. Standard training only disseminates policy, procedure and culture. It actually robs you of making a substantially higher income. Today's restaurant training must include customer engagement and social media management training in order to make the most money the easiest way possible while providing the best customer service.

If your restaurant has only standard employee training how can you deliver superior customer service and above average tips 100% of the time? Standard employees experience their customers as a stream of nameless people who come and go. At the end of a meal and take the 20% left to them, instantly forget everything about that customer, and simply move on to the next one.

If you use my techniques, you'll create kind, caring customers who come specifically to be assisted by you...over and over again. They won't be anonymous, they will become friends and contacts who will get to know you, appreciate your efforts recommend you to other nice people. They will praise you to superiors, help you get bonuses, raises, promotions and give you substantially more than a

20% tip while raving about you on Yelp.

While it might seem like a no-brainer that it's better to be fully appreciated for your unique style and higher paid for your work than to be a virtually invisible and interchangeable servant collecting a standard tip, I often get resistance from actors, singers, comics, and other stage & screen performers.

They feel uncomfortable putting substantial effort into their waiter jobs when it's something they're doing just to pay bills until their careers take off.

If this applies to you, please know this feeling is fundamentally unhelpful, for several reasons. First, the principles I'll be teaching you about becoming a superstar waiter can also be applied to becoming a superstar performer.

Think of your restaurant as a theater. All your fellow waiters are on the same stage; but you're going to turn the audience members into fans of you specifically. As you build your personal fan base at the restaurant, these audiences will be returning over and over again to enjoy more of your performances...and the special memories that only you are providing them.

Also think about what an incredible advantage in attitude this gives you from your peers. The vast majority of performers resent their day jobs, and so they tackle them grudgingly, exerting the barest amount of effort needed and no more. After they've spent most of their time filled with negativity and a closed heart, and actively avoiding giving their restaurant audiences an extra special experience, how well do you think they're going to do when they're at an audition for a huge role? How much of a positive attitude and superstar vibe do you think they'll be able to muster when it counts most for making their dreams come true?

Plus you never know who's going to wander into your station. Sometimes you'll get customers who can actually help your performance career— especially if you're working in a major entertainment center such as New York or Los Angeles. How much more likely are they to do that if you dazzle them as a superstar serving them? Another factor is very straightforward: money. Why wouldn't you want to make a lot more cash at the job you're already doing?

It's common for performers to spend hundreds of dollars on courses such as "The

Business of Acting" that end up having little or no effect on their lives.

If you follow this book's advice, it'll have a dramatic positive impact on the business you have now and the future business you are working toward. You will also earn more and have more freedom and energy for the things and people you love..

Finally, you'll actually have more fun at your day job following my techniques. You'll fill your station with customers who haven't simply wandered in off the streets, but are fans coming to enjoy you and your special gifts for making an event and controlling the outcome. Then again, if you aren't currently striving to work in show business, you may find my techniques give you so many opportunities you may find yourself well positioned to go into just about any career.

Either way, you should never feel that you're "betraying" your dreams by turning your job into a happy, fulfilling, and lucrative daily experience. If you're truly committed to a career outside of a restaurant, then you don't need to be miserable to make it happen.

On the contrary, the more you nourish yourself with positive energy, more and more "supporters" and a growing bank account, the more likely you are to achieve everything you're going after.

I remember the first time I realized I had created my first customer for a book I was writing when I was standing at the front desk of The Brandy Library where I had taken a part time job in order to pay my bills while I wrote.

I was writing feverishly when one of our regular customers came up and asked what I was writing.

I told Larry it was a book on better customer service through name recognition in the hospitality industry and how to easily get a customer's name and use it. He thought for a moment and said, "You're going to need to change the title but I want a copy."

I remember being confused by the statement. "What does one have to do with the other?" I asked. "I'm in real estate." He said. "And your book is needed in every industry but if it says "Hospitality" my employees won't read it." I was in shock.

Here I was still writing and because I had created a regular customer who felt comfortable talking to me about my interests outside of the restaurant I had my first sale! I began to look at all the customers in Brandy Library quite differently. And assist them any way I could.

Question:

How can you see yourself benefiting from having more connections, more energy and doing less actual work? List 5 ways this will help you.

How do your customers become "Regular" customers right now?

Chapter 2:

Creating an Experience

Are you trained to sell products or to provide a customer experience? When personal computers first sold to mass audiences in the 1980s, they were all pretty similar—gray, text-based, and focused on delivering functionality.

Then Apple came out with its Macintosh, which looked more like a work of art than a data cruncher; and which focused on not only getting a job done, but on providing a memorable experience carefully crafted to make people happy every single time they used it. A similar situation exists today in restaurant service. Most waiters are trained to be nameless, interchangeable servers who perform a straightforward job of delivering food and drinks, and otherwise are instantly forgettable. What this book will teach you to do is become the waiter equivalent of an Apple Macintosh (or iPhone, or iPad, or whatever your favorite device is).

You'll be serving food as efficiently as anyone, but you'll also be creating a wonderful experience for your customers, fueled by your unique personality and style, that will make them want to come back to you over and over again.

You'll start off treating every customer who comes to your station like a VIP. You'll find some people don't merit star status, and that's fine; you'll simply refrain from using your customer retention techniques on them. For the customers who you find do deserve your special care, though, you'll be empowered to hold onto them. After you do this for a while, your station will be filled with returning customers who appreciate and reward you for being extraordinary, and for making their every visit a special one.

Over time, you'll find that making your customers feel like VIPs will make you feel like a superstar. You'll also find that trying to make every meal a memorable experience will make your time at work creatively challenging and fun...and very financially rewarding. One experience I remember creating while I was testing out theories for this book: Will customers tip much more for an extraordinary experience?

This was a tough one as I was hostessing and not really in the position to receive the tip so I deflected to my colleague "J."

Now I had just titled my new chapter "Creating an Experience" when the phone rang. It was a customer hoping to make reservations for she and her five friends to celebrate her boyfriend's birthday. BIRTHDAY! Ding ding ding! The alarms in my head went off! I had to think of a way to test my theory quick! After a brief hold, I was back on the phone asking questions and

helping her visualize an evening like no other. Suddenly her simple query of, "and can you put a candle in a dessert?" became the easy pickings for great information like: the birthday boy's name, age, food & drink preferences, her name, her learning my name, telling her that the server could bring out a special spirit bottled the year

of her boyfriend's birth and that he could shoot a quick surprise video. The women on the phone was astounded by all that could be taking place and couldn't wait to come in and meet both of us. Meanwhile "J" had NO idea what I had been up to but decided to go along with my test when he discovered it was all in an effort to see if his customer might tip more.

Well long story short the evening was a huge success a dessert plate was mad with the boyfriend's name written in chocolate, the guest arrived asking for me by name, a short, one of a kind video of the happy birthday moment was made, photos we took went viral with "J's" name credited with the extraordinary efforts made and the best part? After mentioning that this was all "J's" planning and executing he was given a 30% tip on a $640.00 check. Not bad for doing essentially nothing out of the ordinary except now it was an experience. Question:

Can you think of some special things you could do for guests who are celebrating? List 5 things you could do to make the event special for your guests:

Does the person answering the phone know what you do that is unique and special?

Could you find a way to make him or her want to talk about your special services?

What other ways could you learn guest's names when they are already at your restaurant? Have you ever thought to introduce the owner, manager or chef to the birthday boy or girl? Do you like knowing the chef or owner when you dine out?

Chapter 3:

Own Your Own Business Within "Your Restaurant Here"!

Being an employee in a restaurant puts you in a wonderfully unique position. You can think of yourself as owning your own business—but with zero overhead.

That is because you don't have to pay for business rent, utilities, food, beverages, cooks, hosts, inventory, maintenance, accounting, or anything else. The restaurant you're in does all that for you. All you have to do is show up within that larger business, and focus like a laser beam on your personal product—which is your service. If you do a great job of creating a unique experiences for customers with your service, then they'll compensate you for it. And the more you grow your business by attracting loyal customers, the more you'll earn.

Meanwhile, you're investing no money in building your business and you have absolutely no risk of losing money only gaining!

How many other jobs let you run a business within a business?

When looked at the right way, this is a sweet deal...if you're prepared to take full advantage of it. I could probably give you a thousand examples of how I have used the resources around me to create an extraordinary, memorable experience for a customer and they have put huge amounts of money in my hand as a result of it. Once I saw a gentleman struggling to read the menu so I brought over, on a silver tray, a pair of red rimmed glasses in a case. (They were mine. I was going through a "red phase" and I was at the dollar store so I bought them, added "For LeeAnne's V.I.P. customers" to the case and quickly made $100.00 off of them the same day.)

Now I could have sent over any one of the more appropriate looking glasses but as the fifty plus year old customer lifted the glass case thankful for the gift of sight in the dimly lit room, I said, "The only catch is that I need a picture of you wearing my glasses on our Facebook page" They all started laughing when the guest opened the box to show his friends the glasses that would for sure create a great photo and out came the cell phones and cameras and a lot more laughter. By the time they left they all knew my name and the host was thanking me for a remarkable evening and that my unique handling of a possible awkward situation set the tone for an extraordinary evening. Suddenly there was a $100.00 bill in my hand and a glowing review on Facebook, Yelp and Twitter. For that moment I was in the cheap eyeglass business and I had spent: $1.00 for a 1000% return.

Question:

If someone gave your friend a fully stocked, fully staffed Jewelry store, rent free in the center of town and said, "sell as much jewelry as you want for as long as you want and keep 20%. Would you think your friend lucky and why?

_____

_____

_____

_____

_____

_____

What if the store didn't have the "foot-traffic" or customers during slow times? What would 5 things could you suggest he do to get "the word out"?

_____

_____

_____

_____

_____

_____

Chapter 4:

Greet Them!

Right now you probably focus only on your section and on whatever customers happen to wander into it. If you want more money and a much easier shift what I suggest you to do instead is be proactive by greeting customers before they get to your table.

I know this runs counter to traditional training. Waiters are taught to stand against the wall with their hands behind their backs until a customer is seated at their station. But seriously, if I walked into your house, would you be doing that? Or would you be saying, "Hey, come in! Let me take your coat!" That's how an owner greets a guest. And as the owner of your business within a business, that's what you should do.

Stay close to the restaurant entrance, and keep an eye out for customers who are loaded down with umbrellas (when it's raining), or bags or packages (especially during holiday shopping seasons), or even heavy coats (during cold weather). Help these customers out as soon as they set foot in the door.

At that point you're not just a waiter anymore; you're a considerate individual who's going above and beyond to be helpful.

Now the customer is almost obliged to have a conversation with you. You can kick it off with, "Welcome! Thanks for coming in. Is there a reservation under which I can check you in?" If the reply is, "Yes, it's Mr. Buckley," turn to your hostess and say, "Ashley, this is Mr. Buckley. I'm going to go check his things. Do you know where he's sitting so I can bring the coat check ticket over to him?"

The hostess probably doesn't know where he's sitting—which is great. Because when she says, "I'm not sure," you can say, "Well, I hope Mr. Buckley is sitting with me"—and then leave!

If you've encountered the sort of customer you want, he's likely to be thinking, "Wow; no one else in this restaurant has helped me with the door. Nobody has helped me with my coat. No one else has introduced me to the hostess. And there's only one waiter who knows my name." And so he'll turn to the hostess and say, "Yes, I'd liked to be seated at one of her tables, thanks."

Now you've got someone at your station who appreciates you for being more than just a waiter. You haven't even taken his order, but you've already established a positive relationship, and a feeling from your customer that he owes you above and beyond your 20% tip.

Another advantage of this "Greet Them!" technique is that during the slow hours, such as the pre-dinner period, it allows you to steer customers to your station who you might otherwise lose to random placement. That means more service, and more tips, every day. Because this isn't typical behavior, your fellow waiters may tell you that you're nuts: "What are you thinking, doing more than you have to?! We never go out of our way to create extra work for ourselves!"

But you know what—who cares what they think? This is about you setting yourself apart from your peers. Because not only will you end up with a bigger tip, but these customers are likely to come back specifically to enjoy more of your VIP service— and continue tipping you big.

While all the other waiters are hoping to get standard tips from strangers, you'll eventually be waiting on a steady stream of customers who you've turned into your fans, and who are coming to the restaurant primarily so they can be served by you.

Once I was walking through Angelo & Maxies on Park Ave South and 19th street. I had only been working there about two days and didn't know the table numbers yet. I saw a hostess going to escort a couple to their table but didn't offer to carry the lady's drink. I think because it was filled to almost overflowing. I saw an opportunity to kill two birds with one stone: learn table numbers and make a guest feel special by having two people assist them. Well, when I saw how gorgeous the woman was I just knew the

gentleman must be feeling proud as a peacock so I put her drink on a tray and lifted it high, Statue of Liberty Style, and let the whole crowded dining room know that I was with a couple of V.I.P.s. Everyone stared, stopped eating, stopped talking . You could feel the curiosity in the room. It was great! When we reached the table there was a busboy pulling out the chair for her after watching this display of pomp and circumstance.

Shortly afterward the gentleman approached me, in front of my boss who now owns Tao and asked my name put $20.00 in my hand and said he had never felt so wanted by a business before in his life.

That was a drink the customer was going to carry to her table herself. I grabbed it, made

$20.00 extra dollars and as if I wasn't already Rich's favorite manager, I was on the fast- track to becoming one! I used the "Statue of Liberty" carry for the rest of my management and hostessing positions by the way and although I can't say to the penny what it has netted me I do know it is around the $5000.00 mark. Think of it. When you carry things in front of you, isn't that what everyone else does? How can you be remarkable doing things the way everyone does them? That was $5000.00 and lots of business cards from people who want to dine when I'm working because I make them feel special. $5000.00 for lifting my arm ten inches higher when I walked

Question: What are some other problems" you could solve for your guests?

Name at least 5:

How can you solve problems outside of the restaurant to gain customers before you arrive at work? List at least 5

Chapter 5:

Exchange Names

Customers are 80% more likely to patronize business when they

are known by name. When I'm providing a service to a customer, I want that customer to know my name, and I want to know the customer's name. This lays the foundation for a continuing relationship. Again, lurking by the door is a great way to accomplish this. When a customer comes in, you can say, "May I check you in?"

The customer might reply, "Yes, my name is Johnson."

Now you have his name. "Hello, Mr. Johnson," you reply. "This is Ashley, our hostess." Next, say to the hostess, "Oh, I hope Mr. Johnson is sitting with me"—and walk away!

If Mr. Johnson responds appropriately by telling the hostess he wants to be seated in your station, then you've got him as a customer. (And if he doesn't, he's probably not the kind of VIP guest you're looking for...)

Once Mr. Johnson is seated, wait until he asks you for something even slightly beyond the norm. When he does, work in your name. For example: "Can I have another napkin?" "Of course! You're in LeeAnne's (use your name instead of mine) station! You can have whatever you want!" or "Can I have an extra slice of lemon?" "Of course! You're in LeeAnne's station! I'll get it for you right away."

Service isn't simply saying "yes" and going the extra mile. It's about doing the unexpected to create a memorable, wonderful experience for the customer.

When you stick your name into your sentences, and make a customer feel he could have had a whole lemon orchard if he'd asked for it because he's at your table, you're giving him a reason to remember his meal...and to come back so he can enjoy another wonderful experience from you.

You never want to sound canned when you provide your name. It always has to come from the heart. If your customers perceive you as authentic, then they'll start using your name—and not in an arrogant, finger-snapping way, but graciously—and you'll have established a lovely relationship.

When that happens, go to the hostess after the customer leaves and say, "Just so you know, Mr. Johnson has requested me as his server." She'll then link Mr. Johnson's name to yours, so any reservation he makes in the future will be placed in your station. That's a customer you now have for life.

There's one more major thing you need to do, though: Make sure you remember Mr. Johnson's name and details. If the next time he comes in you don't recall his name, that'll be worse than if you never learned his name in the first place.

Of course, because you'll be meeting dozens of new customers a week, it'll be nearly impossible to remember each of their names without some help. So during your next break, in either a paper notebook or mobile device, write down Mr. Johnson's name, the date and time he came in, which table he was sitting at, a brief description of him (height, weight, hair color, type of clothing—whatever will help you remember him), and anything notable about

your time with him (e.g., his food preferences; for more on this, see "The Dollars Are in the Details" chapter). This written record will be a lifesaver whenever Mr. Johnson returns—because you'll be studying your list of names every night, and doing your best to memorize each key customer.

Something else to do when you get home is back up your list. If you've written your information in a paper notebook, transfer it to a Word document on your home computer. If you've typed it into a mobile device, copy that file to your computer. This information is gold to your business, so treat it that way by always having backup copies. Finally, if you care to go the extra mile, briefly search for a photo of Mr. Johnson via Google Images, Facebook, or Flickr.com, and add that picture to your profile of him. That might sound like a lot of work, but if an image is available online you can usually find it in a few minutes, and then copy & paste it into your Word document in seconds. If you're like most people, you'll find it easier to recognize Mr. Johnson the next time he comes in when you have his picture right next to his name and description.

If you follow the advice in this chapter week after week, your station will be filled with steady customers who are there to specifically enjoy you, make you feel special while you're making them feel special, and tip big. Meanwhile, your fellow waiters will be standing around idly and just hoping some strangers who walk in are assigned to their tables.

Question:

What are some other ways you can learn the names of guests? Name at least 5:

How important do you think it is to a guest to be called by name and recognized and why?

List at least 5 guests you know by name and their drink and or dish of choice:

Chapter 6:

Thank _YOU!_

Are you sending the wrong message? Even a "Thank you" can convey thanklessness. Really "Thank" your customers and watch customers return much more frequently! Many restaurants train their staff to respond to both a customer request and a customer's thanks with "Absolutely!" I vehemently disagree with this— because that response makes it sound as if whatever you've been asked to do is nothing.

If a customer says, "Can I have an extra slice of lemon?" and you reply "Absolutely!", it dismisses the effort you'll be making—and that's neither accurate not helpful to you. It's effectively saying, "I cut lemons and bring them to tables all day long, whether you're here or not."

It is some effort to go into the kitchen and cut off another slice of lemon. Maybe the chef is pissed off, and he's like, "What are you doing in here? You're taking up too much room!" Maybe there's a long walk from the kitchen to the customer's table, and while passing a different server's station another customer flags you down for a favor. You sliced and delivered the lemon specifically for your customer; and you deserve to score points for it. Hospitality isn't pretending that you're doing nothing. It's about letting your customers know that you are doing something for them, so they can feel special and cared for.

So what do you say instead of "Absolutely!"? In response to the request, get your name in. "Of course! You're in LeeAnne's station! (using your name rather than mine). I'll get it for you right away." That tells the customer you're ready to go above and beyond for her because you're special, and you'll always treat her as special too. When you deliver the item and the customer says, "Thank you," respond with "Thank YOU!"

That's effectively saying, "Yes, it was an effort; but thank you for being here." And it's also saying, "Thank you for letting me provide this service to you...because I know your tip will reflect it. Thank you in advance for that bump above 20%." Whether the customer subconsciously picks up on both meanings or just the first one, at least you're not dismissing your effort with a robotic

"Absolutely!" (as in "No problem! I love cutting lemons!"). Even a polite "You're welcome" is dismissive, because it's so instantly forgettable ("You're welcome, I do this all time, and it's as automatic for me as this response..."). A reply of "Thank you" isn't the norm, and that makes it stand out.

And what you want to do as a server is stand out from the crowd— albeit in a positive way that affirms how special both you and your customers are.

One of my favorite things to say to a customer when they say, "How are you?" "Better Now!" or "Better now that you are here!" It always makes them laugh or takes them by surprise in not being made to feel average but absolutely wanted. By the time I do anything for them and the respond with, a thank you, my reply of "Thank YOU!" is heard as sincere appreciation for their patronage and their business. Try to love making people feel special. They work hard for their money too and when they feel appreciated they are more likely to spend it with you and tell friends to do the same.

Practice saying "Thank *YOU!*" instead of just plain "Thank you"

for the next two weeks inside and outside of work. Who will you

say "Thank *YOU!*" to tomorrow? List 5 people:

Your bank teller? The girl at the grocery store? The man who gives you your coffee?

What were the different reactions you received after saying, Thank

YOU!"? (List 3)

Chapter 7:

Leveraging Your Incomplete Party

You have an easy opening to create special, lasting relationships and memories when assisting the first person of an incomplete party. This is a great opportunity to get or give names, find out what the occasion is and even start planning a photo to be taken and posted. Customers will frequently rendezvous at your restaurant—which means one of them will arrive before the other (for a couple) or others (for a group). This common situation

is referred to as an "incomplete party"—and it's an opportunity for you to take what you've learned so far to another level. Let's say the first to arrive is Ms. Reed, and she's meeting two male business associates. Because you're using the "Greet Them!" technique, you've greeted her at the door; and because you're using the "Exchange Names" technique, you've already gotten Ms. Reed's name.

Now you have an opportunity to take things a step further. Once she's settled, pass by again and say, "Ms. Reed, I know you're waiting for some colleagues. What are your guests' names? I'll tell the hostess and make sure that you all connect right away."

It's possible Ms. Reed will decline your offer, saying, "Oh, don't worry about it, I'll see them when they come in." But because you've already extended her some other courtesies, she's more likely to say, "Their names are Mr. Marston and Mr. Winston. Thank you."

This is your chance to reply, "Thank you. My name is LeeAnne (substituting your own name). If you need anything, please just ask for me."

At this point, the chances are Ms. Reed is thinking, "Wow, this LeeAnne really knows how to provide service. I'm going to sit at her table."

Meanwhile, you definitely should tell the hostess, because Ms. Reed's colleagues might arrive at a moment when you're busy serving other customers, and you need to keep your word. But if you happen to be at the door when someone new comes in who fits your expectations—in this case, a male businessman—don't hesitate to go up and say, "Oh, are you Mr. Marston or Mr.

Winston?" With luck he'll reply, "Why, yes, I'm Mr. Winston. How did you—wow, thank you! This is service." You can then reply, "I'm LeeAnne, and I'll be taking care of you tonight. Right this way, Mr. Winston." Then bring him to the table where Ms. Reed is waiting and pull out his chair for him.

And repeat this process when Mr. Marston arrives.

You now have license to use the names of all three customers for the rest of their dining experience— and establish a relationship with each of them. For example, as you're walking by, even if you're busy, you can just casually say, "Ms. Reed and Mr. Winston, how's that steak? It's amazing tonight, right? They must have gotten those cows from Heaven!"—and then walk away! What you're saying to everyone else in the restaurant is that Ms. Reed and Mr. Winston are VIPs. Both of these customers will appreciate that.

Then on your next pass by the table, say something positive about Mr. Marston's dish so he feels included too.

If you do little things like this throughout during the meal, you're likely to get higher than 20% for your tip—and because there are multiple people at the table, that'll add up. Finally, when you can grab a few spare minutes, jot down the names and descriptions of all the customers in the party—because it's possible any or all of them will come back another evening to enjoy more of your special brand of service and you'll need to be able to remember the name of each one. (I am a big fan of the old fashion, black & white composition books. The pages never fall out and guests assume you are in school.)

When I was managing, I could not emphasize this "incomplete party" trick enough. It created so many regular customers it wasn't even funny. To keep them focused on getting and remembering names, I used to have a game with the staff: whoever could name the most customers in the room won my services for one table during the rest of the shift. Of course it was always the server who had the most incomplete parties who always won and of course they always had me wait on the table they liked the least but it always turned out great. Learning and remembering and using customer's names became the culture of the restaurant, regular customers were warmly welcomed, wanted to learn more and help with the private ambitions of the servers they grew to know and I could assist the guests that may have slipped through the cracks. (Plus, as is often the case it was usually a misunderstanding and with a little finesse the "least favorite guest" turned into great customer and regular for the life of the restaurant.)

Please purchase a composition book in the next 24 hours and from this point on point on any time an incomplete party arrives in your station please write his or her name in the book with details such as date, weather conditions, appearance (Politically correct please. You never know who's eye's may end up looking at your book when you have it for months or even years. Don't put in ink anything you may regret later.)

How many customers can you greet by name right now?

Do you know the occupation, spouse's name or any interesting detail of any of these customers? List as many as you can below:

_____

_____

_____

_____

_____

_____

_____

_____

_____

_____

_____

_____

_____

Chapter 8:

Meet thy Neighbor

Do you know the owners of your neighboring businesses? You should! Those business owners are asked daily to recommend everything from drinks to experiences. If those business owners knew you by name they would be sending customers right into your station every hour of the day! Until now I've been focusing on customers who happen to come into your establishment. You needn't restrict yourself to walk-in business, though. Like any entrepreneur, you should attract customers using every option available to you—and there's a whole world right outside your restaurant.

The next time you head for work, leave an hour early and take some time to explore the neighboring stores and services in your area. What you'll probably find is that there are businesses all around you serving hundreds of customers daily.

And what you want to do is start steering those customers your way.

Your best opportunities are with vendors whose service complements yours. For example, if there's a convenience store that sells coffee and donuts every morning, it's getting a steady stream of customers who are used to buying nourishment in the area. It won't be a big leap to persuade a certain percentage of them to try out your restaurant.

Also look for stores that target the same type of customer as your establishment. For example, if you're working for an upscale restaurant catering to business people, look for places that sell elegant suits, or high-end handbags, or thousand-dollar shoes. If you're working at a restaurant promoting natural ingredients, look for health food stores, juice bars, and fruit & vegetable stores. If your restaurant caters to those who love the arts, look for nearby bookstores, music stores, movie theaters, stage theaters, and comedy clubs. Give yourself a week or more to explore your area. As you do, make a list of the places that attract the kind of customers you're after.

Also, if you don't already have a stack of the restaurant's business cards, grab them now. start visiting each local vendor on your list, and try to develop a personal relationship with the owner and/or staffers.

For example, if you drink coffee, consider buying it from the coffee & doughnut shop that has hundreds of people streaming through it each morning. After the owner has gotten to know your face, come in one day during a period when her business isn't busy and strike up a conversation. "Thank you so much..," you might say, "You know, You guys help me get through every shift and I would love to thank you in return! I work in the restaurant across the street. If you are ever looking for a great place to eat, please come see me, LeeAnne (substitute your own name)." Write your name on and hand over your card, ask for his or her name and

make sure you remember and use it the next time you are in.

If being that straightforward makes you uncomfortable, though,

here's another way to go. Start off by complimenting the people and the product they're selling: "You guys are so nice to me. And your coffee is so great, it gets me through the day." Then work in what you do: "I'm always running around at my restaurant, right across the street. Your coffee is my fuel. Maybe I can do something for you in turn." At this point pull out your card.

"I'm LeeAnne. If you ever want to come in between 5:00 and 6:00

pm, before we get super busy, I will totally hook you up. And if you have any customers you like who you want to send over, I'll do the same for them. Just tell them to ask for me and to mention your name. I'll make sure they have a great experience too." Write down "Come between 5:00 and 6:00 pm for special service" on the back of the card, then hand the card over and ask "What is your name by the way?" and be sure to shake hands.

Notice that you haven't promised anything crazy, like buying someone dinner. You've simply pledged to deliver something beyond the norm—a memorable experience. And that's what you want to provide to everyone.

Also notice that you're instructing the vendor to have people mention not only your name but her name. On a practical level, that helps you keep track of who's sending you the most business, so you know who to keep encouraging. But beyond that, it makes the vendor feel good. If you give her the sense that her name carries weight in your restaurant, then she feels like a VIP—and who doesn't enjoy being made to feel special? Further, notice that you're steering business to fill your slow period. If you've got more customers than you know what to do with during lunch and dinner hours, it doesn't really help you to get in more customers then—let alone ones who expect special treatment. But if they come in during a period when you otherwise wouldn't be earning a dime, then not only will they be super welcome, but you'll actually have the time to give them extra attention.

And once the great job you do gets back to the vendor who recommended you, she's likely to send yet more customers your way.

Another benefit of this strategy is that the customers you get through it are likely to be on their best behavior. After all, they've been referred by someone who they probably see and conduct business with frequently; and you can report on them just as easily as they can report on you. The fact you all share a mutual acquaintance provides an incentive for everyone to impress each other. What do all these extra customers and local good will cost you? Just some inexpensive business cards; and the time it takes to cultivate positive relationships with the store owners around you so that they effectively become your local marketing campaign.

I once bought a train ticket for someone when the ticket machines were down & he had no cash. I had cash and he was about to have a really really bad day. I stepped in & said I would buy it. In his utter confusion I put my business card in his hand as he was saying, "But how will I return the money to you.?" I just smiled and said mail it to the address in your hand and walked away. Not only did I get my money back, he also enclosed a

$4,000.00 gift card for Tiffany's! Alright, it was really just a

$15.00 gift card for Duncan Donuts and in a very sweet hallmark card but it felt like a million bucks and that's one more person sending people down to ask for me. (His train ticket was only $12.00 by the way. It's not like I am curing any diseases or anything, I'm not that sweet. I'm just always looking to increase business for my boss and maybe me someday but this is a really good habit to get into.) This is networking and you will be doing it any business you go into because your contacts are your revenue source.

TIP: Conversations with strangers: Always try to find a way to say, "by the way if you send friends in, just tell them to mention your name so I know to give them VIP treatment." EVERYONE WANTS TO THROW THEIR OWN NAME AROUND!

Question:

How many "Your Restaurant Here" business cards do you have on your person right now?

How many people do you talk to in a week? 20? 40? Imagine if all 20 of those people sent you 1 referral customer who left a $20 tip. Could you use an extra $400.00? Those people that yo talk to also talk to other people. People who are looking for great food and service. Your business cards are little keys that unlock money for you and conversations for other people you do business with. Name 20 people you do business with every week:

Have you asked your friends and family to send you customers? Probably not and in all likelihood they assume it would make your job even harder waiting on more customers when in fact those would be the easiest, most polite customers you serve. Isn't it

ironic that in not asking those closest to you to send you customers, you actually have less energy and less money for those you love. Their referral customers are always nicer, bigger tipping customers due to the relationship with the referrer. What are 4 ways you can get friends, loved-ones, priests, mailman, parents, uncles even your children sending you customers?

Some restaurants have their own social media departments but at "Your Restaurant Here" you can always share and tweet what they we post on Facebook and even mention specials and events. Pictures go a long way to bringing in new customers who are friends with the people you connect with and with twitter and Facebook a picture of a vacant table with "Last table available! Your should be here!" written on it could inspire a whole "new seating" for your section with just a few taps.

Getting friends to share and "like" what you post is as easy as mentioning them or tagging them in a picture. "Jenifer West, wouldn't this pumpkin pie look great on your tongue right now?

You do like pumpkin pie right" or "JK, you taste-buds called and asked for this....(Picture of Chef's special) when can you bring them by?"

If you can post and tweet, what are some fun and engaging things you can say, do, post tag and or share? List at least 10. Ask friends and family for help to get really creative. (The time to think of what to post is now, not when you need customers.)

Do more brainstorming during family meal to get your income on autopilot fast!)

10 Quick social media ideas:

Take pictures of food creations and the chef! Tag the artist at work and his masterpiece. You would be surprised how fast it gets shared with his networks! (Or maybe you won't be surprised!) Let's face it if the chef does this himself, he is bragging. If you do it you are smart and recognize great talent. Big difference. Take advantage of it! Take advantage of ALL the free marketing tools you have in the restaurant! If people are creating... use it. If people have egos... use it. Make the most money the easiest way possible using Everything around you "snap it, tag it, mention your own name in it and post it." Tell people they'll get something special when they sit in your section. (They will of course. They will get you as their server plus just ask the manager to send dessert or an appetizer from you. Jennifer and Jeremy will be glad to accommodate and very aware of the fact that you are promoting their restaurant!)

Chapter 9:

The "Hook-Up"

Become invaluable to your customers!

Quite often, your customers completing their meal isn't the end of their evening; they'll want to do something afterwards. If you ever hear one of them saying, "Gee, I don't know where we should go once we're done eating," consider it a golden opportunity.

You should be prepared to tell them, "There are some great choices tonight. There's a sample sale just next door, a poetry reading down the block, a rock concert eight blocks south, and a dance club two minutes from here that's kind of exclusive— except I can get you in with a phone call." If you can organize something for your guests—and especially if you can promise them VIP treatment and/or access to something relatively exclusive— they're going to see you with new eyes. Suddenly you're not only their waiter, you're a concierge with connections who holds the keys to their perfect evening.

Of course, this requires that you keep up with what's happening in your city. But you've already taken the first steps for this in the previous chapter, "Meet the Neighbors." By exploring what's available in your neighborhood, and introducing yourself to the owners and staffers, you've begun to form valuable bonds. You can now take those connections to the next level.

Scout out nearby locations again, but this time with an eye on evening entertainments that might appeal to your customers.

Whenever you find one that appears to be a good fit, approach the owner or manager, and offer to refer customers from your restaurant in return for their receiving some sort of VIP access or treatment for them. Because you're in a position to send over dozens of customers monthly, many owners will (correctly) view it as a win-win situation for everyone involved.

Do yourself favor and call ahead to let the business owner know that your VIP customers are coming over. Always put any seats or tickets in your name not the customer so it gives everyone involved one more reason to use and remember your name.

Also make a habit of starting each morning reading about events in your city. For example, major cities such as New York, Los Angeles, San Francisco, Chicago, Boston, Miami, and Las Vegas have their most notable events described by local editions of Time Out Magazine, as well as by daily newspapers.

Don't ignore blogs and websites, either. If you live in New York, for example, the finest source of daily updated live comedy information is

BestNewYorkComedy.com, which is entirely free; the best free sources of discounted Broadway and off-Broadway tickets are TDF.org and BroadwayBox.com; and the best source of cheap access to theater TheaterExtras.com, which for $99 a year lets subscribers see select off-Broadway and Broadway shows for a mere $4 per ticket. If you literally make it your business to keep up with what's happening in your area and around town, it'll pay off for you in concierge-level tips. I typically make these kinds of "Hollywood hook-ups" a couple of times per night; and not only does it substantially increase my income, but it helps ensure that customers keep coming back to me for new suggestions and connections.

Don't restrict yourself to the world outside your restaurant, either. You can also make impressive hook-ups using the people you work with every day!

Specifically, if you have a table that's celebrating and/or spending a lot of money, and the manager walks by, say, "Oh my gosh! Have you met the manager, Elaina? Elaina come say hello to Marilyn. It's her 21st birthday, so this is a landmark night for her!" Meeting someone who can send dessert and champagne from you plus has time to take pictures will be the perfect highlight for them, make them feel really important but also takes pressure off of you so you can leave the table to greet other guests. it makes everyone at the table feel like celebrities with insider access.

Who doesn't feel special sitting at a dining table and having the manager or owner standing by making small talk? Make your customers feel more like bigwigs and they are apt to tip more. Why not make more and work less?

Question:

What are some of the events and happenings in your town, community, area? List 6 events, exhibits, shows, readings, sales etc.

Could you see how a newspaper with arts & leisure section, events & entertainment section, sales & coupons, news releases, local oddities etc. could help to make your customer feel like a V.I.P. and more likely to put more money in your pocket?

Question:

When you call ahead to let a local business know that you are sending your V.I.P. customer over, who's name should you make the arrangements under and why?

When was the last time you called a manager over to introduce them to guests in order to get away from a table and catch-up on putting in orders, mise en place, run food or greet new guests? Could you communicate to a manager from across the room to come over? Would you find a way to if you knew it meant more money to you and the restaurant?

Chapter 10:

Paying Attention

Paying close attention to your customers may seem like such obvious advice that you're wondering why I'm even mentioning it. But I can tell you from long experience that very few waiters actually do this well.

For example, I'll notice a customer is shivering, or has just put on

a jacket while inside the restaurant, because she's been placed right next to a drafty door. I'll go up to her and say, "I hope you don't mind my noticing, but you seem cold. Would you prefer another table?"

Along the same lines, if I see customers frowning, I'll walk by to eavesdrop. One time the snippet of conversation I caught was, "This is awful. You can't see anything from here." I didn't hesitate to say, "I'm sorry, but I couldn't help overhearing. If you like, I'll be very happy to place you at a table with a much more interesting view."

I can't tell you how grateful these customers were—and how ridiculously they over tipped me later.

Not all problems stem from the restaurant. But that doesn't matter; when guests are in your station, your job is to help them out with whatever they need.

For example, I've sometimes seen customers fidget and come over to learn that they've run out of cigarettes. "Simple!" I tell them, "I'll have a pack delivered for you in about five minutes."

"Really?" they say, looking overjoyed. "Of course, just tell me what brand you want." Because I've scoped out the neighborhood, I know precisely who to call that delivers cigarettes; and when asking my customer for the money to pay the delivery person, I simply tack on an extra $5 for myself for the service. There are hundreds of different reasons for individual customers to become unhappy. What matters isn't the particular cause, but your noticing the discomfort and letting them know they should never feel trapped or stuck when you're around— because you'll always find some way to offer them new and better choices.

Question: Give 4 examples of problems that can be made into relationship building solutions and how:

_____

_____

_____

_____

_____

_____

Was one of the reasons simply that by returning more than two or three times, you or your co-workers began recognizing them? How else could you create a regular customer? List 3 different ways:

_____

_____

_____

_____

_____

_____

Chapter 11:

Leveraging Special Occasions

When you see customers obviously dressed for a special occasion, carrying gifts or flowers even pre-ordering a birthday treat this is the time to start talking about a photo or video (which will go viral!), helping with after meal activities and arrangements (which creates an unforgettable impression of you), getting and giving names which will "stick" and create a repeat customer for life.

When you see customers arrive dressed up in some special way, or carrying flowers, or loaded with gifts, this is another great opportunity for you.

Go up to them as soon as they walk through the door and say, "Wow, this looks like a special occasion! Tell me, what's going on?" The chances are one of them will be happy to reply, "We're celebrating our wedding anniversary!" or "It's my birthday!" or something comparable.

Without hesitating, respond, "That's wonderful! I'm so excited for you! Tell me, what's your name?" This is actually an unusual question for a waiter to be asking. But if you deliver your response in the right tone, you create a vibe that you're celebrating with them, so it's only natural you want to know the name of the person whose special day it is.

After the customer answers with something like, "Oh, I'm Megan," you can proceed to say, "I'm so excited for you! I'm going to make your night super special."

At "Your Restaurant Here", we LOVE giving away a free dessert to really take our guest's dining experience to the next level where most restaurants do NOT.

Since this is a special occasion, and your table is feeling extra happy, this is a moment they'll want to preserve—so offer to do that for them!

Say, "This is so nice! Can I take a picture of you guys?" The usual response will be, "Oh, yeah! Please do!" If they have a camera, offer to take it from them so they can all be in the shot. If they don't, use a camera that you've made a habit of taking into work for precisely moments like this one.

Once you're holding a camera, you have a lot of power. So say to them, "I do this conditionally. The first way is your way, but the second way is LeeAnne's (your name's) way!" Now you've injected a bit of fun suspense; plus you've reminded them of your name.

On the first shot, they'll probably do what everybody does—hold up their drinks, smile at the camera, and be sweet but kind of boring.

When that's over, say, "All right, the second way is LeeAnne's way. And if you like how this comes out, I want you to post it on Facebook!"

With that extra bit of anticipation created, position things so whatever special event plate or candle you've created for them will be in the shot. Then tell them the following: "This is your rock star cover photo. You have to point at the camera and be angry rock stars." Point the camera at them and say, "Angrier! Angrier!!" This is so much fun for grandparents, or anybody that age, because they grew up in the 1960s and 1970s when angry rock stars were at their heyday. Besides, everybody's got a little rock star in them. When your customers are sufficiently going "Arrr!", and sticking their fingers and/or tongues out, take the shot. (Or take several, and then show them the best one.)

Chances are they'll love it, because it's so different; no one's directed them to pose that way before. So repeat, I want to see the funniest one on our Facebook page!" Now add, "Feel free to mention that it was taken by LeeAnne, world famous server and photographer at (name of your restaurant);" if they are having a great time you can even say, "Awww! You guys are so cute! I

want a picture with you!" Holy cow! Most times they want this too they just haven't thought of it. Now they get to take a very personal, special part of the restaurant with them into their social world: You!

If they follow through, these photos will be an advertisement for you for the thousands of Facebook friends of each person at that table. Imagine that you do this several times a day. You'll soon have your name requested by the thousands, your station on "serious cash" auto-pilot; and it'll have cost you only a few extra minutes per table.

But you don't even have to stop there. To take things to the next level, carry around a small, portable device that can shoot short but high quality videos. You can then also preserve your customers' memories using motion and sound! You should get your manager's permission for this. But assuming you receive a green light, you can tell the hostess that whenever customers call in to reserve a table for any sort of celebration, she should ask if they'd like their event preserved by a 2-minute video, at no extra charge. Most people will be thrilled to say "yes." To make your life easier, have the hostess add that for the best results they should come in during non-rush hours (e.g., 4:00 pm-6:00 pm). And to encourage the hostess to be your partner in this, tip her something (say, $5) every time she gives you a party during the pre-dinner period. (Your small incentive might spur the hostess to ask everyone who calls, "By the way, are you celebrating anything? Because we have a great videographer on staff...")

As a result of your efforts, you'll automatically be assigned some of the most joyful customers the restaurant will have the opportunity of hosting—and you'll be making them extra happy by preserving their celebration forever.

For example, one evening a customer named Bob wanted to come in and celebrate his girlfriend Lisa's birthday. I started with the camera pointing at me saying, "I'm LeeAnne, your server for the evening. Over there is Bob—he's waiting for you, Lisa. Bob's created a really cool birthday event for you." I turned the camera on Bob, who said, "Hey Lisa! We're going to have a great celebration tonight!" And then I cut.

I also shot a short scene when Lisa arrived; treated Lisa with extra consideration during the meal; and included in her dessert a chocolate-drizzled "Happy Birthday, Lisa!" and a lit candle. Finally, I shot Lisa making a wish and blowing out the candle. Lisa assumed that Bob had arranged every detail, and was highly impressed with how thoughtful he was—but the truth is it was all my idea. How grateful do you think Bob was? Very. And his tip expressed it.

But that's not all...because I was the one with physical possession of the video! So when I was able to get Bob alone for a few moments, I said, "Let me get your email and your Facebook address. I'll upload the video to your Facebook page; or, if your settings don't allow for that, send you the link so you can "share" it to your page and have Lisa see it. I just want you to promise that if you like it, you'll mention on Facebook that it was shot by your waitress LeeAnne."

Notice that I'm not asking Bob to mention the name of my restaurant. I'm also not mentioning it in the video. That's because, unlike photographs, videos contain spoken words and so raise liability issues for the restaurant. In addition, a high-quality restaurant probably won't want to put its stamp of approval on a low-res and rushed video. However, when I post the video to my Facebook page I'll include tags that let people find me on Facebook— and so learn where I'm working.

What all this means is that in addition to getting you a huge tip, your video can end up creating thousands of dollars' worth of free Facebook advertising for you.

Question: What are some ways you can tell that people are getting together for a special reason? List 6:

_____
_____
_____
_____
_____
_____

What are a few of the ways you can make your customer's dinner really special and memorable at no cost to you or the restaurant? List 4:

_____
_____
_____
_____
_____
_____

What are 3 ways you can make sure your customers remember your name?

_____
_____
_____
_____
_____
_____

Chapter 12:

Know Your History

Do you know why your boss started his business? Some history of Soho, the buildings even residents? You would be surprised how you would be able to create regular customers with interesting facts and highlights but due to standard training only offer only, "Sparkling or flat water?" as conversation starters.

In previous chapters I've had you discover what's in your neighborhood and what's happening around town. But it can also be helpful to know the back-story of the very restaurant you're working in.

Many Soho addresses have colorful histories. Some have had famous politicians or movie stars dine in them. Others have been the scenes of dramatic clashes or calamities. Whenever your owner has some spare time before or after hours, ask for any interesting stories about how the restaurant came to be, and if it played host to any memorable events.

Don't stop there, either. Find out if the building the restaurant is in, or any building nearby, has historical significance.

And learn and share with guests any wonderful stories you discover about Jennifer or Jeremy and why/how they built this business.

You can even ask them how they choose ingredients or the each wine for this current menu to see whether there is a story to tell. Guests are fascinated that they live just two blocks away and are here every day, built it together over twenty years ago and raised a family while doing it.

While verbal anecdotes are likely to be your best source of information, don't restrict yourself to them. Google Soho, and its key players, and jot down anything that strikes you as fascinating.

When you're looking for ways to break the ice with new customers, these tales can be of immense value. For example, one time I seated a couple in a corner, and they asked, "Oh, can't we sit by the window?" I already had a request for the window table so instead I replied with an air of mystery, "You don't know about this place, do you?" "What!? What are you talking about?"

"Well, that table by the window is the scene of the biggest mob hit in New York." This was absolutely true. "Only certain really brave people are willing to sit there." This was a bit of an embellishment on my part; but I wanted both parties to be happy with their tables.

My customers were instantly hooked and wanted to know every detail—while seated safely away from the window. I shared with them the dark story, and they were riveted. Their experience was transformed from a mere meal to living in the shadow of a jolting event that they'd remember for the rest of their lives.

How many people do you think they referred to me? And how many more do you think came in from the referrals of friends of friends of friends?

Never underestimate the power of a great story.

Question:

What are some unique characteristics about the area, town, building, menu, restaurant, Jennifer and Jeremy?

_____

_____

_____

_____

_____

_____

List 3 different ways you could use this information to engage your customers:

_____

_____

_____

_____

_____

_____

Could you also use this information outside of the restaurant to draw people in? Would your banker dry cleaner, book, jewelry, children's store owners find it intriguing? Could you use this information in order to get these business owners to ask for you for a business card from you? How would you do it? What would you say?

Chapter 13:

Manage Introductions

Every now and then Jennifer and or Jeremy or one of the managers will have friends or colleagues in to dine. If these guests are seated in your station, you'll be able to do a better job if proper introductions are made upfront.

Let's say the guests are friends of the Mark the manager. The usual, but wrong, way for Mark to bring them to your table is to say, "This is LeeAnne. She will be your server tonight."

The right way to do it is for Mark to say, "This is LeeAnne. Have you ever dined with her before? LeeAnne, these are my friends John and Sam from college."

On the surface it might seem like a small difference, but it's actually huge. The first introduction makes Mark the host and you an employee who works at "Your Restaurant Here". But the second introduction elevates you to being Mark's co-host, and gives you permission to address his guests by name. This creates a much more relaxed and personal relationship. It also makes Mark'sguests feel more like VIPs—because they aren't being served by a random server, but by someone Mark is treating as his peer and co-host.

If you feel you have the kind of relationship with management that allows you to request this, then simply take the pertinent person aside when things aren't busy and say, "Can you do me a favor and introduce me personally when you have your guests at my section? It'll help them feel more at home if I start using their names right away and when they feel welcome to use mine. Plus I want them to know they can ask me for anything, even when you're not at the table or not here if they return."

If you put the request in terms of being able to serve their esteemed guests more effectively, you'll probably receive a "yes."

Question: Can you think of anything you could do in advance of the manager/owner's guests arrival that would make the evening remarkable for them and actually save you time and effort?

List at least three things you could do:

_____
_____
_____
_____
_____
_____

Was one strategy introducing the manager, owners or sommelier? How does this save you time, energy and effort?

_____
_____
_____
_____
_____
_____

How can you also create a social media opportunity from these introductions?

_____
_____
_____
_____
_____
_____

How could you use this opportunity to create a V.I.P. regular customer?

_____
_____
_____
_____
_____
_____

How could you use a business card to offer new customers services like "Pre-ordering" or chef's pairings which are not on the menu?

_____

_____

_____

_____

_____

_____

Chapter 14:

The Dollars Are in the Details

At every given moment you could be creating a regular customer simply by focusing on details. Standard training does not accomplish this but try to teach yourself to focus on the smaller details all around you. Take note, for instance, of everything surrounding your customer's experiences, what the chef is preparing, sales in the neighborhood and you will have limitless, excellent tipping, consistently referring, social media posting friends. Friends who are a joy to serve and who look forward to supporting your employee.

This chapter offers a variety of additional ways in which you can go so above and beyond the norm as a server to ensure your top customers keep coming back to you...and compensating you like the star you are.

In the "Exchange Names" chapter, you learned it's a great strategy to jot down and memorize customer names. If that's as much as your memory can manage, then stop there, because it's much, much worse to get a fact wrong than to never bring it up in the first place.

If you have a mind that's great at recalling details, though—for example, if you're a stage performer who's practiced at memorizing pages of dialogue— then be more ambitious about the amount of customer information you retain.

For example, imagine that the first time Mr. Howard and his friend

Ms. Jennings come into your restaurant, you use the "Grab Them!" technique to check their wet umbrellas and coats, and the "Exchange Names" technique to get their names; and you notice their preferences for their steaks and salads.

Now imagine that because you did a great job of serving him, Mr. Howard returns a week later on a sunny day. You spot him again as he enters and say, "Mr. Howard! It's so great to have you back!"

First point scored: You've remembered his name. You then add: "Thank goodness the weather is nicer and you don't need your umbrella today." Second point scored. Mr. Howard realizes you're paying close attention to him as a customer.

Next, you ask, "Will Ms. Jennings be joining you today?" Third point scored; you remember his dining companion.

Smiling at how you've made him feel special, he replies, "No, actually I only have a short amount of time today. I'm just running in to grab some food before returning to the office for a meeting." "Then I'll try to get your food ready for you as soon as possible. Would you like what you had last time—steak medium rare, and a Waldorf salad?" Now he's grinning. "Yes, that'd be great." "I'll go tell the kitchen right now. And I'll tell them to give it top priority."

Wow. Your customer hasn't even touched a menu, and you've practically got his order cooking. After you've served his meal and he's getting ready to pay the bill, you add, "Mr. Howard, in case you're ever in a hurry again, let me give you my Google Voice text number. You can just text me "The usual, 6:00 pm," and I'll have your medium rare steak and Waldorf salad ready for you. Or if you're bringing in a guest and need something special in advance, like flowers or a certain kind of chocolate on the table, just text me. I'll make it happen, and you can reimburse me when you arrive."

Wow! You've just elevated your relationship with Mr. Howard from waiter to personal assistant! Naturally, you'd make this offer only for customers with whom you have an excellent relationship, and who you fully trust to reimburse you for whatever they request. You can add an extra charge for this type of service, so when you order flowers or chocolate or whatever you need through your network of contacts, you'll be making extra dollars on top of the handsome tip Mr. Howard will be providing for his meal.

The next time Mr. Howard returns, you're busy at another table so don't get to see him come in. Because you told the hostess weeks ago that he's one of your regulars, though, Mr. Howard is automatically seated in your station. (Of course, even if the hostess messed up and tried to place him somewhere else, Mr. Howard would insist on being served by you.)

You greet him enthusiastically as usual: "Mr.Howard! How wonderful to have you back!" He doesn't appear to be in a hurry this time, so while you're ready to rattle off "steak medium rare and a Waldorf salad," you simply ask, "What are you in the mood for today?"

Mr. Howard replies, "I'm torn between the steak and the lobster. What you do think?" If you were an ordinary waiter, you'd simply say, "They're both excellent."

But because people are often tempted by more than one entree, you've previously requested from your manager the ability to let top customers order a combination dish. This isn't something you could do on your own; but thanks to your initiative, and management's blessings, it's another way for you to provide extraordinary service: "Well, Mr. Howard, if you like, I can get you a plate that's half steak and half lobster. That choice isn't on the menu; but if you'd prefer it, I can make it happen."

Mr. Howard happily agrees. He adds, "That's such a great option! You know, there are lots of items on the menu that are tempting, but I'm wary of taking the chance of ordering them in case I won't like them."

Because you've also heard this before, you've discussed it with your manager too; and he's provided permission for you to say the following: "Actually, if you ever come in on a Tuesday between

4:00 and 6:00 pm, I hold a tasting party that allows customers to try a range of our dishes and wines for a flat fee. "And by the way, if you come in on a Thursday between 4:00 and

6:00 pm, I can offer you and your guests free champagne with your meal! "Those are both normally slow periods for the restaurant; but because of these special offers, my station is pretty full at those times. That makes my manager happy, and my VIP customers like you seem to appreciate it as well, so it makes me happy."

Customers enormously appreciate such options, and they aren't terribly difficult to provide; but very few restaurants actually offer them.

Mr. Howard replies, "You know, you're an angel on earth. Whenever I need to relax and not worry about anything, I'm coming here. And when I have a colleague or friend I want to impress, I'm also coming here...to be served by you."

Now that's what great service is all about. It's not screaming

"Absolutely!" every time a guest asks for something.

It's paying strict attention to your customers, and keeping an eye out for anything out of the ordinary that you can do for them that will make them feel cared for and special. Remember, as a waiter you're a small business owner with no rent, no inventory, no employees to pay, no business insurance, and food that's prepared by other people. That's a good place to be. And it means you can focus 100% on raising your service to the level of superstar. Of course, not every customer rates superstar treatment. But if a guest starts snapping his fingers or whistling for your attention, speaks to you with disrespect, or simply fails to compensate you adequately in tips, you can always gently cut that customer loose. All you

have to do is provide that person with standard service, and no more; and let the hostess know that the customer is no longer a request of yours, so should be placed randomly at whatever station is next available.

The customers that treat you right, however, are your personal VIPs or PPXs

The other servers in your restaurant are waiting on strangers who walk in, eat, and leave. But you're getting in regulars who know your name, and understand that you're unique; who appreciate all the extra things you do to make them feel welcome and special; and who are happy to reward you. The result is your station is continually buzzing with warm feelings.

When this happens, how much more enjoyable do you think your experience is on a daily basis versus that of your colleagues?

And if you have your heart set on a career beyond your restaurant, how many potential doors do you think you're opening by handing out your business card around your neighborhood and spreading your name around town; and by having so many loyal, appreciative, and affluent customers?

Also, how much more performance experience and star charisma do you think you're developing by serving a large audience of fans every day? Finally, bottom line: How much more do you think you're earning in tips?

Money is freedom. It buys you time and options. If you become a superstar waiter, the odds are great it'll ultimately help you become a superstar in the career of your dreams.

Question:

What on the menu or in the restaurant is of particular note to you? What deserves its own spotlight and applause? Is it a food item? A drink? The Wine list? The type of cuisine?

_____
_____
_____
_____
_____
_____

What are 3 different ways you can let people know about these restaurant highlights?

_____
_____
_____
_____
_____
_____

Chapter 15:

Create Postable Experiences

Are you creating postable, sharable customer experiences?

Because of social media your restaurant visibility is now global not just local.

Because of social media your marketing dollar will go one hundred times farther than just two years ago.

Because of social media your restaurant, your promotions and pictures of your edible creations are on the phones and screens of tens of thousands of hungry customers (Sometimes before the dish has even left the kitchen!)

What are you doing to match employee training with this new landscape called Social? Does your business and everyone in it need to supply a more sharable, postable, "Tweetable" customer experiences? If you are going to thrive you do!

• Do you love being at work and creating these moments?

• If not you should! This saves you time in the long run and brings you great customers and more control over your station.

See how to "get more" from giving, sharing the business with vast amounts of potential customers, creating and sharing photo opportunities with guests, food and the business. Learning to doubling their tips and your sales at the same time!

Question:

How can you capitalize on holidays and area events to create and promote little

"Tastings" at tables in your station during off peak hours?

Who can help you create and run profitable tastings which essentially run themselves and easily become social media opportunities for the restaurant, the customer, the Chef, the Somm and you!

How could you publicize a tasting table?

_____
_____
_____
_____
_____
_____

10 Free Clientele Building Tools To Coach You Can Use Right Now!

#1 Employees: Don't poison yourself. The people around you may not actually want to be work so most of what comes out of their mouths is going to be disparaging and unhelpful. Whether you want your job or you are pursuing other passions, your goal in showing up at work is make as much money as possible and be treated with the most respect. So, don't pay attention to the negative it can ONLY bring you down and your job is hard enough! (And what you don't realize is that many of these people may want you to be down like they are and if your goal is the most money then you really don't have time or head space for their crap) We all know the job is stressful, customers don't understand, most managers are tough and you co-worker is never around! Your focus should now be tuning that out & taking the first customer

#2 Names! From now on, every opportunity you have to get someone's name USE IT! People feel much more inclined to shop more and "gift" when the person helping them knows them by name and uses their name during their time in the store. Some of the ways you get your customers names are: If they are looking at/for special occasion items, if you recognize them from being in before, if you've seen them in the neighborhood or introducing

them to your boss or telling them about events or happenings in the area that they may not be aware of. Any way you can strike up a conversation and introduce yourself, the guest will usually introduce himself and if not, now it is perfectly normal to say, "Sorry, and your name?" Being able to call someone by name is very powerful. Whether he is your guest or not he soon will be and the customers around him want to know why you know him.

(This makes getting their names easier too if the opportunity presents itself

#3 Employees: You have your own small business! You have a turn-key operation that you don't have to stock with inventory, furnish or pay rent for! This is a opportunity of a life time! Suck every single benefit from it. You work in a place that you don't have to create the product or invoice the user. Try to focus on getting every single customer and every single dollar and then leaving. You will feel much more in control (As you should since you are really the master of ceremonies)

#4 Sow Seeds in the neighborhood of your small business. Talk to all the business owners and employees in the neighborhood as you do the things you usually do, just start introducing yourself as well! Everyone in the neighborhood should know who you are and what you sell so that everyone can refer you.

#5 What's in your wallet? It should be 5 business cards. (And you should do this for the rest of your life!) – Plan to give out 5 cards a day even if you leave the customer service business. This is such a good habit because you begin to talk to and listen to people differently. The bank teller, the deli guy, mail man… You will be surprised what happens when you start saying , "oh hey, I never gave you my card… any time you want to come down or send friends in, just tell them to mention your name and I will totally hook them up! Thanks for always taking care of me." (Hostess, drycleaner, bartender) Just wait and see what kind of service you get next time you go in there! This is all about building a foundation for your section. A foundation on auto-pilot filled with people who have been referred by friends or neighbors! You are not an anonymous employee, you are Mark or Ashleigh "who is going take really good care of the people I send in." And if the guest comes back to "thank" me you can bet I'll will send more! Not only that, the guests I send in know that you are an acquaintance of mine. That we obviously talk. Have a good relationship. That's why they are getting the hook up. These customers will not want to jeopardize the relationship that was built and therefore will be extremely patient and respectful customers. You are now controlling the type of customers you are assisting!

Hmmm… "Thank you so much for your help! I'm going to tell all my friends to ask for you!" Yeah enjoy that being said 5-6 times a day just for taking out a business card! Imagine if you actually did talk to 5 people a day giving them cards & writing your name on them and the "best" time to come in for super V.I.P. attention (Haha.. say anything here. You don't want to be caught with your pants by offering anything free or anything you can't deliver on. But when they come in you know there are ways you can upgrade them and make them feel that V.I.P. land only exists with you.) But if you gave 5 cards out in one day and each neighbor sent one person in who wouldn't have been there in the first place, let alone early, that would be 5x a polite and courteous exchange with people coming in and asking for you personally.

*Say for instance that you work lunch. Let's say for example an average tip is $10.00. Now you've got your neighbors putting $50.00 in your pockets before the rush even begins! Now what if all of those guests felt like it was more appropriate to leave $13.00-$15.00 dollars? Well that's $65.00-$75.00 instead before the night even starts. If that was happening every shift and you had four lunch shifts a week, this one tool alone would put $260.00-$300.00 per week or $13,520.00-$15,600.00 a year in your pocket.

$15,000.00 more a year just for saying, "Thank you for my coffee! Hey you guys are so nice to me whenever I'm in here! I work across the street!" (Or downtown it doesn't matter) instead of, "Thank you" or, "Milk, no sugar."

Saying, "Hey thank **_YOU!_** You should let me treat _you_ to something sometime. My name is LeeAnne by the way (Extend hand to shake here! No one will ever refuse and they will remember you forever.) What was your name?" Remember his name. (You will need it trust me.) Now launch back into, "I would love to repay the favor so if you come down or send friends down make sure they mention your name so I can do something special." Be vague but be clear that you A) appreciate their kindness B) now know them by name and will C) do something special for anyone they send in. That's a loaded hand shake and you may not even have a business card to give them…uh-oh you'll just have to drop it off tomorrow which is when you reinforce this whole concept one more time AND ask for his business card. If this near "Your Restaurant Here" do ask if they deliver, or pick up. If you are speaking to the business owner he knows that that means more money in his register. It is really important to start thinking about your daily interactions and how you can use them to fill your small business early so you can make money & go home early. Even if you tell people you are only going to be there for a year before your side project is done or you are finished with school… all that means is that they better hurry up and start sending people because it's not everywhere that friends can stop in and mention his name. And people love having cache like, "Mention my name and Joe will take really good care of you." I look for that opportunity now every time I answer the phone at work.

How many of you have a business card for "Your Restaurant Here" in your wallet right now? Is the restaurant becoming empty around 8:45? Business cards will change that! Anywhere you go you can drop a card on someone saying, "You guys are the best, I love your…Muffins, candles, clothes, discounts, cars, burgers, services (whatever!) let me give you my card and anytime you want to stop in I would love to treat you like a super-star! ..If you come in early I can give you the royal treatment." You can VIP them in so many ways! Maybe by introducing them to the manager or suggesting you take a photo of them etc. You have so many free tools that will make a guest feel special, wanted, valued and want to dine at "Your Restaurant Here" more often. And when I say free tools please know that I never mean up-selling or refolding a napkin for someone. You have real tools, money making tools, all around you always at your disposal but no one in the restaurant business is going to tell you that because they think bringing amazing food to the table and refolding a napkin should be enough for a guest to think, "I am coming back here every week and I want this guy to always be my server!" Sorry, we are never going to build a repeat clientele foundation with a folded napkin and the best fish ever. The world is social. Everyone is now focused on building relationships Start thinking like a social media hub and you will become your own $2000 billion dollar Facbook of the restaurant industry but trust me it takes business cards and looking at each person you meet outside of the restaurant as someone you want to give a business card to.

I once bought a train ticket for someone when the ticket machines were down & he had no cash. I had cash and he was about to have a really really bad day. I stepped in & said I would buy his ticket for him. In his utter confusion I put my business card in his hand as he was saying but how will I return the money to you. I just smiled and said mail it to the address in your hand and walked away. Not only did I get my money back, he also enclosed a $4,000.00 gift card for Tiffany's & a new car! Alright, it was actually my money and a $125.00 gift card for Duncan Donuts and in a very sweet hallmark card but it felt like a million bucks and that's one more person sending people down to ask for me. (His train ticket was only $12.00 by the way. It's not like I am curing any diseases or anything, I'm not that sweet. I'm just always looking to increase business for my boss and maybe me someday but this is a really good habit to get into.)

This is networking and you will be doing it for almost any business you go into or stay in because often your contacts are your revenue stream such is the case here as an actual frosting on the cake you already have in your section which your boss and his marketing / PR arm has provided.

TIP: Conversations with strangers: (Especially people in the restaurant biz.) Always try to find a way to say, "by the way if you send friends in, just tell them to mention your name so I know to give them VIP treatment." EVERYONE WANTS TO THROW THEIR NAME AROUND!

Making more money and doing less work is easy. It just takes remembering people's names, looking for incomplete parties, walking guests out and putting them in cabs when you are not busy. It is taking pictures but "styling" for your customers and asking them to put it on the AG Facebook page. It is thinking outside the box to blow someone's mind and make your life easier and easier every day.

#6 Managers work for you! (They just don't know it yet!) Start introducing all your regular customers to your manager and make your life easier! Use his title and prestige for yourself. Why should he have all the fun? It will impress your customer to know the boss personally, make you job easier and cast you in a very favorable light once your boss sees the extra effort you are making to get to know the neighbors. (Don't forget to write their name down in a book somewhere though! Once you know someone's name it is very important for business that you don't forget it.

#7 Pictures & Videos = $$ In so many ways! Look for opportunities to take your customer's picture. When they try something on or hold something up say, "Oh, You should instagram that!" You will be blown away by how fast they start posting and asking you to take their pic in different outfits or holding your products. When you offer to take their picture tell them that you do it conditionally: "First the way you want then the way I want." (Or "First Your way Then Mine.") 100% of your customers will be intrigued, even excited by the prospect and wonder what you have in mind. Take the first picture with them posing the way everyone has posed since the beginning of time. (Yawn) Then tell them "Ok, now it's my turn… this is your rock-star album cover and you are angry rock-stars pointing at the camera. " If you sneer and point at them as an example they will mirror you and do it back. Everyone has a little rock-star in them trying to get out and this is the perfect way to help let that rock-star out of them. As you are setting up the picture you can mention,

The other part of the condition is if it comes out good, you can mention me when you post it." Having the opportunity to do something completely different will make them putty in your hands and whether they post it or not they will ask you for your name.

You are the master of ceremonies and you have the reins after all! Send and include "Every once and a while I host private fashion shows, test drives, tastings for my customers. Would you like me to e-mail you when I have events or specials?"

#8 Help parents! Entertain their kids. It frees them up to shop and endears you to them. Just start talking to the kids. Prepare ahead of time with songs, games, stories, coloring books. (Your co-workers will think you are insane. Your boss will think you are brilliant and all the moms in town will be asking for you personally! Then start using mom's camera to take pictures of "junior" doing cute things and get them together for photos with your products in the pictures and watch how fast her tweets, and pictures make you employee of the month!)

#9 Make Calls On Your Customer's Behalf! Do you know about a concert, book signing, cute pair of sandals on sale, sample sale, new restaurant with amazing calamari? When you are talking with your customer about why she is shopping listen for important details that you can use to further assist her and get her name at the same time. Would those sandals match her dress perfectly? If she is interested then make a call to that store down the block to have the sandals set them aside for her. Then ask her name. When she gives it to you don't feel like you have to share it with the other store. They should only know your name. The name of the person sending them a customer (And perhaps they will eventually return the favor!) Now you got her name, provided unheard of customer service that she will tell friends about and the store down the street knows your name and make refer you customers. Not bad for noticing what's on sale in your neighborhood and what your customers are wearing!

10 Grab it! Gab anything and carry it. Help open the door, grab an empty stroller to assist a mom.. Grab bags. People walking in with bags may like to leave them some place safe to free up their hands while they shop. Simply reach for their belongings (This is really easy if you know their name. .)… "May I carry your bags to your table?" (Or check your coat for you?")

Training Employees: How To Train For Higher Sales & Lower Employee Turnover

Servers, Bartenders, Bussers *And* Hosts Or Hostesses: how you train your fellow/new employees will directly impact your income and how hard you have to work every day. Would you like to correct fewer mistakes, enjoy a fun upbeat team environment and have a more solid co-workers supporting you? It's all in how you train the new hires.

Training is everything and the more you train new hires to appreciate your restaurant, it's owners, managers and it's team, the more you are actually training them to support you, make money FOR you and bolster you when you need help. If you train new employees that yours is an average restaurant with short comings, has short tempered co-workers, short sighted managers, bad staff meals, inconsistent or slow kitchen staff, inattentive or micromanaging owners or managers, and ignored equipment repairs, you will actually be doubling your own work load and you don't even know it. You will actually be training your new team to bring you down when you need to be brought up.

If you incorporate eye-rolling or sarcastic remarks in your training you are actually teaching any new hire to work less, feel unenthusiastic, sell less, create short-cuts, look for ways to create smoke or text breaks instead of keeping side-work, customers and sales flowing or ever helping you when you need it. You will make less money and work harder when you train with indifference or disdain. New hires will be less effective and less productive and actually cost you time and money if you highlight anything but the very best of the restaurant. You actually now control the mood, the spirit and new income of the entire restaurant when new employees are in your hands. You should not take this responsibility lightly.

Showing new hires the tricks to check your phone mid-shift, chew gum, be disrespectful to managers or stand in front of a computer when you have no orders to put in instead of helping to run food or drinks or engage new guests in order to book future reservations speaks volumes to the person you are training and the people watching you. When your new co-workers do these things, they will find themselves in "hot-water," eventually let-go and you will have to start training someone new all over again which means twice as much work before you to get a team-member up and running and contributing equally to the pool. Attitude is everything and if you want the absolute most money (even if you only plan to be in this business for another week, training new employees to appreciate all of the amazing things about your restaurant, training them to constantly look for something to do, restock, run, clear, carry, double check or find a customer to engage with and get a new reservation will directly create an environment of positiveness, support and more sales. Your new employee can make sure you make more money and guarantee you that you are always are welcome based on how much effort and energy you put in to each conversation with them. Leave the negativity, the side comments and bullying to people of less caliber who may just be going through "something" or on their way out themselves and focus on the new way to make more money by supporting, exciting and teaching team-members to be their absolute best. Isn't that what you want for yourself? To be the best and make the most money? Then train your new employee that this is the absolute best restaurant to work at, these are the best people to work with and Jennifer and Jeremy are the best people to work for. The systems that they have in place here make it easy to make money, unlike most restaurants this is a well-oiled machine and when all the parts move together it creates amazing experiences, money, friendships and feeds your future dreams. Jennifer and Jeremy's generosity makes it easy to reward customers that you like and who tip well so that you can make even more money. Their attention to detail and quality creates a constant flow of customers. While other restaurants come and go, try and fail, offer discounts and Groupons to get customers through the door, be better. Be the best. Help create an ever growing clientele with your supportive, enthusiastic, high-caliber training to create bigger spending, nicer, repeat, regular, effortless, fun customers for your team' future.

Train for the best, expect the best, be the best. How you do anything is how you do everything and training the people around you to create money, time and wealth for you is what the smart people do. Not so smart people create animosity, hardship and ill-will for themselves and the people around them and subsequently cost themselves money. Create the best for yourself by being the best for your restaurant.

What are some of the really unique and positive aspects of your restaurant, neighborhood, menu, culture, owners, managers, clientele etc.? Write them below so you can share them with fellow employees and make your life better/easier and more lucrative!

_____
_____
_____
_____
_____
_____
_____
_____
_____

Thank *YOU!*

I think when we employees think and feel like part owners and partners in a business, everyone wins. I hope this workbook helps you to make more money and create easier and more lucrative shifts for yourself and your coworkers.

- L.A. Homsey – Bartender at The Trailer Park Lounge, NYC

646-687-5572 Leeanne_homsey@yahoo.com

Begin With Any Of The Steps On The Bottom. Use 1, 2 Or All 5 For A Week And You Will Be Well On Your Way To Creating A Really Lucrative, Easy Customer Base For Your Section.

In A Few Short Weeks You Will See More Money, More Relief At Work And More People Who You Know By Name And Will Follow You In Any Business.

"Grab It" - An opportunity to get your guest's name and make additional tip + get the hostess to start working with you!

"Questions" - "Special Dinner?" "Special Occasion?" "Work In The Neighborhood?" "Are You Going To The Sample Sale/Show/Book Signing Down The Block?" - An opportunity to surprise dessert, photo/video or refer you. customer for added benefit for dining with you

"Get Your Name In It" - An opportunity to get your customer something for them.

The Hostess, Your New Best Friend - An opportunity to get referrals to your station because you offer a special video you hear about the sample sale? ship of the birthday dessert surprise. Guests may even tip the host for this info

It's All in a Name - So know them. Knowing the customer's name opens the door to bigger tips and non-verbal communications from anywhere in the dining room. Every photo or video request by your customer is an V.I.P. Saving time means big money when you can turn additional tables. Customers who you know by name are also easier to serve and are more patient. When you learn a name be sure to record it in your book w/ his food and drink preferences so you can greet him personally guide him to your station & make him a "regular".

"Man About Town" - Read up on what is happening and use it "Did you hear about the sample sale? a movie? Book signing, New guano bar? Cooking class? App?

"Hollywood Hook-Up" - "What's the plan for the rest of your night? I can and get you in get you a car, get you to the head of the line." An opportunity to share something "not on the menu" and have guests remember your name

"Thank You!" - An opportunity to remind customers you've just done around you to refer guests to sit in your station.

"Meet The Neighbors" - An opportunity for business owners around you to refer guests to sit in guest's names

"Social Media" - Harness the new frontier of the internet by helping your guests make your station viral. Every photo or video request by your customer is an opportunity to go viral. Use your HHH phrase to get guests posting your name to all of their friends. No one will want to sit ANYWHERE else and the best part the hostess will have to push reservation times earlier & earlier as your station fills.

"Know Your History" - What is the history of your restaurant? The building? The Owner? Google and ask! This is an opportunity to share interesting facts w/ guests for more customer experience + $$

"Introductions" - "Have you met my boss? The Chef? Steve, the General Manager? Amy, the Sommelier?" opportunity to bring the guest into the restaurant community and "belong." Guests are more likely to return to places where they are known

"Incomplete Packs" - An opportunity to get, record and use your guest's names

"Special Orders Don't Upset Us" - VIP guests you know by name can call you if they need special attention: Flowers on the table, appetizer on the table, req, a specific able or order everything ahead of time. This special service is only available with you and they know it

"Manage Introductions" If your manager know's someone's name have him introduce you for a better introduce you for a better

Start Use any of these to start your guest on the $$$ path

"Text Number" - Give this Google # only to your good customers to use "in a pinch." They'll feel like you are their man on the inside!

V.I.P.